IMAGINING THE FULL HUNDRED

Imagining the Full Hundred

by

Fiona Owen

ISBN: 1-903314-60-7

Published with the financial support of the
Arts Council of Wales

Cover illustration: Malcolm Strongetharm

Published and Printed by
Gwasg Pantycelyn, Lôn Ddewi, Caernarfon, Gwynedd LL55 1ER.
Printed in Wales

Contents

For Gorwel
Fy Nghariad

You cannot go high enough nor low enough nor far enough
to find those whose bowed and broken beings will not rise up
at the coming of the kindly heart, or whose souls will not shrink
and darken at the touch of inhumanity.

J. Howard Moore

With thanks to my dear Mum and Dad, brothers Gavin and Malcolm, and Aunty Pat for their bottomless love and the blessing of our shared lives together; to the *teulu annwyl* I have married into; to Shula, the point of love between; to my precious circle of friends, for their continued support and encouragement (big thanks and love); to David Hart & Paul Matthews, poets whose relationship to the word have inspired and oriented me; to John Powell Ward and Liz Ashworth, whose work I have entered and journeyed with; to Randolph Ellis for his talks on the tonal and fragmentary; to the MA tutorial team and my peer group at University of Glamorgan, whom I worked with from 1995-97; to the Arts Council of Wales for granting me a writing bursary; i Maldwyn Thomas a phobl Gwasg Pantycelyn; and, always and unfailingly, to my husband, Gorwel.

Picnic on Ajman Beach

Was the sky really red? Day sky,
　　but growing plum-purple like night
so we must pack up quickly.
　　A shamal is coming, Father said.
And yes, I could feel my skin
　　prickling with the whipped up sand
and the bay was a bowl of water
　　tipped to slopping over edges.

Sand stings with a wind at it, and my legs were bare,
so I must hop on the spot.
　　　　　　　　Mother had her arms full
of baby boys and was heading for the car when the man
came from across the beach, his robe flapping.
　　　　　　　　　　　　He was old,
like the Ancient Mariner, with the same beard and eyes.
Salam alaykum, he said, and Father spoke back, picking up
the ice-box and fold-up chair.
　　　　　　　　My long hair was twirling
in the tug-chase wind, and maybe I said *Come on, Daddy*.
Then I was aware of the old man's stare and the way
his hands waved over me.
　　　　　　　　No, no, Father laughed,
and went to go, but the fisher man grasped his arm
and told my father *camels, gold, a dhow* like a rime
with a ring to it.
　　　　　　　　Sand was in my eyes, my ears
and I was grinding my teeth on it. The whole world
was graining into sand-storm and, somewhere in the frame
was me, smalling to a speck enough to get blown away.

Mother (who can't swim)

Coming up for air, I see you at the shoreline
circled by black rubber and thick glass.
Within this frame, you are central,
you are sudden, you are unnerving,
you are stamping on the spot as if in tantrum,
you are running circles, you are running a figure eight.
Your hands flap like wet rags in a wind.
Your face is turning itself into throat.

Yards of ocean separate us.
Sea is spilling from my ears.
My mouth is full of mouth-piece.

Then your sound comes
skimming over the water like a flat stone:
it is almost too high to hear.

The Dog Shoot

Sunday morning and we woke to the pop-pop of guns.
Across the stretch of sand, near the Bedouin village,
a Sharjah soldier had a shot dog by a back leg,
one of the pye dogs that we fed.

There was a whole heap of them, chucked
into an old oil drum on the back of a lorry.
Most were not quite dead. Wet noses
stuck out all uneven, paws paddling the air
as if in safe dreams. The whole drum heaved
like a can of caught worms.

We scampered about the compound
tripping in the sand, fetching dogs in
until the house was packed out with those saved.
Then we pounded after the truck, waving our arms.
My mother fell on the subca track and split
her seventies tight pink pants from seam to seam.

Stonefish

Pablo got stung
        messing about in the shallows
where the seaweed was.

We gathered round
        as he gave us his palm:
a small green-ink stain,

tattooed to his life-line.
        Pablo's father shouted Spanish
when he saw it,

brought the mother running
        with a half-moon of melon
still in her hand.

The car left a trail of dust
        hanging in the air,
and the day seemed suddenly becalmed.

When you lived in Jamaica, Mum

I

You were resting on the vast bed
in the middle of the afternoon
where you soon fell into a humid doze.

Small hairs stuck to your damp forehead,
the smallness of your neck gathered beads
of sweat. The unfamiliar heat drained you.

So you didn't notice the scorpion
making its clinging way across the ceiling;
upside down, it couldn't hold on.

Perhaps that's when you woke,
its small weight enough to stir you:
you froze when you saw it.

Strange how he came just then
or did you scream? He grabbed
at scissors. Snipped off the sting.

II

I have this image of you
waiting to cross a dusty road
in Montego Bay.

Your arms are bare and ballet-thin,
and your fawn fifties skirt
falls to mid-calf.

You look left, then you look right.
As you do so, Richard Widmark
drives past in a black car

and he waves.

Cousin in a Strange Land

She was dead when I saw her three friends
huddle up the path towards the front door
which I of course opened, already arranging
my face for the impact. I said, has he found her
and they – one of them – said yes.

She was dead then, when her three friends
closed me into a sympathy circle, my blonde hair
losing its bounce. They said it was okay to cry, while I
burrowed for answers, deeper than they could reach.
How, I said. The valium, they – one of them – said.

So she was dead then. And her three friends
made me tea as if I was in Wales, in the cups
I'd laid ready for her return. Tea is never the same
in other countries. When he found her, she'd been dead
seventeen hours, they – one of them – said.

So, she was dead. And all her friends gathered
among her house plants, wearing white fitted suits
and white lips. He stood at the centre, with their child,
now his. The most beautiful women in Texas
live in Dallas, she'd – once – said.

She was as dead as dead when I saw her,
lying powdered against white satin. Outside,
it was over a hundred degrees, a white heat.
A white noise hissed in my head. I can't live
without him, she'd – once – said.

Rock Fancies Movement

Rock fancies the movement of bird: the flap
of wings, the lift-off, the flight. Rock
fancies taking great strides across pasture,
feeling light among buttercups. Rock
likes to ponder the prospect of stretch
and run, the notions of *fast and feather-weight*.

Sometimes,
after a big build-up,
rock manages a moment of budge.
It comes as a shock, bouncing the Richter scale.
Roads rip, rivers rise. The valley thudders in surprise.
Rock wants to join in the celebrations, but grin has set into gorge.

Rock pauses.

Sonnet for Gorwel

Today you went away for one long week's
summer school. At the station, we pressed ourselves
together, trying to cram lost time into speech
that went nowhere near far enough. A tiny screw fell
from my sunglasses – a distraction. You picked it off the floor
and then the whistle blew. I couldn't use
the sunglasses to hide behind any more.

The studio door is locked and I refuse
to wash the breakfast dishes for the two
of everything. I've loads to do. Time goes by
without you. I'd rather it passed with you
closer, within touch or the flick of an eye.
Each night we'll count the days off down the phone
to Friday, the day you're coming home.

After your leaving

After your leaving, the house began to weep.
The kitchen sink cracked and let water seep
among the dusters, bleach and surface cleaner
in the cupboard below, where the pipe-work leak
swelled up the Brillo pads and ran their corner
to rust. Even the bathroom tap grew nearer
to break down, its washer gone slack,
its drip-drip a plumb reminder
of your corporeal lack.

And now, as the night does its black
thing, and the roof timbers creak,
and I, in our bed, practice the knack
of sleeping alone, I feel my own weak
moment coming on, your pillow beneath my cheek.

Môn Storm

I want this rain this streaming grass these sycamores
stripped this gale this grey
                                 I want to be
held in here holed up let the world whirl

Let the wind
                            snatch paper from tumbled bins
wind it into trees bump the walls and eaves
I want the sky
                        down a bit black a bit
                        left no white in it
wetter is better
for fretting for getting
down into missing you

The world's a whorl
the whole day's a girl
weeping for her love

In Real Time

Water is mud-brown, but who cares?
The canal winds for miles and it's May,
hot enough to burn your nose.

Somewhere between two Cheshire towns
I say: *We are happy*. Hedgerows are lush.
There is play of green and all the world seems

spilling over. Here is no planet ailing.
Away from the car, the squeezing of our Information Age,
we can dream body back into thrive.

In our real-time togethering, we are swans-on-the-glide,
loving the same field, its acreage of ploughed loam.
In the photo I take, your sunburn shows,

your brow furrows as you squint, your hair is unmowed
hay, your stubble grows gold, while behind you,
the earth-field stretches over the hill.

When you shave
you make
your top lip shape
into a beak.

Your bird-face
breaks me into the laugh
I can't help but show.

Your this-time creature face
knows itself watched,
and being shy and rare

alters to the spread of wings
and takes to air.

Your beard

at night
it is a forest
I lose myself in

it is rich foliage
and earth-after-rain

makes me maiden makes me
wander deep after slug-spoor
lichen smudging
sap staining
the white of me

your green
your leafage
your *locsyn*

I am lunar
lying among roots
and leaves
in the vegetable world

a
silver
shiver
of
yin

You are red
sun rising
twigs in your hair
and all the seasons
root you

Moondance

The moon trailed fingers along the banister,
then swung in the long window to watch,
while the woman whirled away from the bedroom door
(where the other one stood in his pyjama top), twirled
over the soft pile so that her nightie frilled out around her,
pirouetted past the bathroom, where the cold tap dripped,
then held a brief arabesque at the head of the stairs,
before launching into her Ain't She Sweet routine
that involved the criss-crossing of arms and legs.

Back she came, leaving a lattice-pattern moonglow
hanging on the air. Back she came, oop-
oopy-dooping, like Betty Boop.
Back she came, slightly breathless,
to where he stood.

She pushed past him, back
into the anxious dark of the bedroom.
He turned and followed,
finding no words appropriate.
The moon hung to listen.
Then, in the hushed house, there came
the small sounds of making up.

Fish

Waking up, I found you changed into a fish,
all old gold and flapping fins. It was a shock
to my early morning fingers: you were cold
where you're usually warm. Your scales
surprised me, but you were, at least, man-sized.

After exploring a kiss, I felt a sense of adventure
come upon me. 'We must employ the pulley-man,' I said,
jumping up and down on the bed. 'He can winch you
to safety, the bath or maybe . . .' (I leapt to the window.
The pond looked cold.) '. . . we could build an aquarium for you.'

I greeted the pulley-man from the upper window,
giddy with excitement. 'You'll never guess,' is what I said.
You chortled from the bed, and flicked your tail
impressively – you seemed to be enjoying
your altered state. I rode the banisters down to the hall,
where I checked my tongue and teeth in the wall-mirror.
The pulley-man flapped the letter box, but I was distracted
by scales, like a patch of eczema, glittering on my cheeks.
Bone was beginning to slip. My eyes were flattening
into silver studs. 'I'm coming,' I called, but the words
bubbled and broke on the air with multiple pops.
I tried the word HELP into the mirror. No sound came.
Then my name dissolved, along with all other words,
and I flipped backwards, out of sight.

Boxing with Shadows

Tonight, the Queen of the Night sings
her wild staccato aria at full blast while I fling

my arms at gargoyles that wink and leer:
Edward Scissorhands has arrived with queer

pincer insect hands. He can slice you in two
meaning to caress. The room is scarcely blue

lit by the cool blue winter moon and still I whirl,
boxing with shadows, feeling myself uncurl

from where I hid, under the covers,
where it isn't safe after all; even lovers

are really on their own and must face alone
the hammering of that top F on frail bone

and skin that dries to dust. There's no one here
but the Queen of the Night, singing a clear
top F (is for Fear). I have perfect pitch, a perfect ear.

Another Annunciation

Perhaps if Gabriel came again to Mary
it would happen at the kitchen table,
in front of her husband, while they were
each sipping tea. Only she would see

the blaze of gold, feel the air waft around her,
so she must shiver at the spread of white wings
and the glory of The Perfect. She would first
feel her heart centre ignite, then the light

would melt lower, until her womb swelled
bright. *My Child* she would cry,
as the flame spread glorious through her
and she would cast her eyes to Heaven.

Joseph would see only her face strange,
shudders of tears then sudden laughter, eyes
changed, magnifying something that was not him.
He would grow afraid of her babblings,

thinking her mind gone. He would tell her
to stop, maybe try to shake her back to him.
My Love she would say, but her words
would fall into cliché. And the Archangel's wings

would whisper away, the tea in the cups gone gold.

That last week

you lay facing north
summer's north
rich with summer's posy

Put me there by the window

You were in that room off the ward
where we could gather by your bed
to wait, to watch breath, wordless
or praying for breath and heartbeat
round the bedside on Thursday night
when we thought: this is it.

But Saturday came you hung on
we kept you earthbound all our circles
of love kept you grounded
and you found a way to whisper

Take me home
                    Evelyn
Dos a fi adra

to that place of trees
the growing pine, the sycamore,
the great orange berberis

Dos a fi adra i Fforest Fach

It was our only miracle
our last hope. When you woke
you found yourself *home*
windows thrown open for air and light
and yes still at *home*
with its polychrome of high summer
petunia, phlox, stock and lobelia
by the window, you were *home*.

Lying in bed, you shed the weight
of world, of work, of all the shocks
that living hearts must take in a lifetime.
Your prayers streamed thanks praise sorrow
tears for the murder of innocence
and *God bless the children*.

You dreamed hieroglyph, far-off temples,
great gold tablets, oceans of white.
You became a shaman, testing flight.

A new light flickered in you

and as ice becomes water becomes steam
you evaporated, slipped the body
one week late, one morning

you became invisible
vaporous butterfly
your chrysalis shed

sloughed off
on the bed your poor lovely skin
and bone empty

left

for all our goodbyes

Aunt

I have been dreaming of you

I saw you come up for air
swim towards that surface where the blue gets lighter
and the weight less crushing, swim up
to that skin that you must break
thin like hymen and as tough

I saw you push through
I thought I saw you do it

Your swimming has been deep
down in how much dark
you can't speak with your cells
so soaked your tongue growing kelp
your blood thick with algae when you try
it comes in a wave of ultrasound
hard to understand your wild slow hand
unable to be fathomed

It is easier to push you back beneath
easier to keep you in the element
you were born in womb-water
they'll give you something to make you sleep
roll you back into your safe sea
out of harm's way lullaby-land, they say

You sink leaden again your ears filling
nose mouth lungs it's like sherry
sometimes, if you have enough
the bottom comes, you know it
it feels like home at least
the shapes their lurking blurred bulk
the slow tidal waft of can't-make-it-out
You'll be still then and silent
used to your own murk

You've tried to creep a-land
I've seen you
take the sky into your eyes
I've seen you
breathe try words sound them
breathe try to make them right
coming up for air
and what little light
you can bear

Your heart struggles now
with the pressure
You hear its pump
sometimes miss
and it scares you
You fear you may dissolve
You float face down
in your own grief

and I dream of you
swimming towards that surface where the blue gets lighter
and the weight less crushing

swim up, my dear
swim up

Brother Francis

We buried the bird and believed that God
was crying with us, for the rain lasted
only as long as the ceremony, which you led
with your pocket-sized *Psalms*.

Serious we were, circle of bowed heads,
hair school-parted, breakfast not yet.
Mummy, why? we wept: broken bird in a soily grave.
She looked to you, small boy, like we all did –

for when you read, your words lit the grey morning,
making the small death matter.

Making tea, November 4th

Look at this keen moon, out already at five o' clock.
A Greenwich Mean Time moon means
tea time keeps its hour, later. At the sink,

I chop and think idly about the colour of veg
and the mildness of November. We say it's wonderful
for the time of year and forget the hedgehogs,

used to deep dreaming by now. The kitchen radio has experts
playing a food quiz. Between them, mellow as mead,
they divide up a cow into portions on a butcher's map,

slice a slither from a cow's neck, cut into the loins,
make off with the rump. Fillet the flesh into neat warm
chunks. Fillet the cow into beef with its heart ripped out.

Look at this moon, run through with a bacon slicer,
lopped gibbous. And a skyline the colour of rare steak.
Bonfire night tomorrow and no need for hot soup or scarves.

Bonfire Night

Bonfire night and I'm in with the dogs.
Alice hides in the toilet. Oscar doesn't:
he charges the length of the house, jitterbugs

at the window, raises roaring comment
with his tail sprung and his body bristling.
Across Llyn Maelog, fires blaze like beacons

or bombed out holiday homes; rockets go whistling
up into sky-night, to burst bellies of light, aliens
to scoff at the stars for one climaxing moment.

A machine gun rattles, there are crackles, pops, and snaps
like over-amplified Rice Crispies. This is a war zone, testament
to all the noise man can make: bangers, fizgigs (lock up your pets).

I am unimpressed by this flex of muscle, this magnificent feat,
this shot-gun display. My mother says they went to sleep
under tables when the air-raid sirens wailed. Erased whole streets.

Hay-making in Capel Gwyn

That was the day
we turned seven acres of hay
by hand.

Don't remember why, now –
                    maybe
the little grey Fergie broke down.

Just the boys and me and that June blue morning
and those lines of felled grass lying
like love-maids' cut yellow tresses.

I had a two-pronged fork
and worked the left-hand stretch of field,
the warm-wood handle worn too smooth for spelks.

However heavy my step started,
I soon grew light in the sun, liked
the near-sounds my movements made:

the clean slip of steel, the sometimes scrape
on stone, the rustle of the cut-grass strands
showing
        a still-green underside.

Oscar

is standing on three feet, his front
fourth paw tucked under his chest.
He looks like he's posing for a portrait,
scenting the air like that, the model dog
poised for action or
                    Plato's perfect dog,
fallen from the Realm of Forms.

And all because of two girls
coming down the lane,
one in a sun hat.

A Heavily Accented Pause

Waiting to turn, a Cheerful Chuckies wagon sits panting,
its load of oven-readies jostling for space, for breathing room.
Beaks and limp jaded feet jut out of side vents at odd angles.
Clipped wings are pressed hard against tender-meat bodies,
clipped beaks clipped to avoid pecking,
picking each other to bits and bones
in the long cramped hours between birth and death.

I can see them all, too close for comfort,
factory-made fodder to be reduced to drumsticks,
wings, giblets, breast, parson's nose, wishbone:
you hold it with your little finger and
make a wish, make a wish, make a wish.

A pair of wild scrambled eyes peer out
between necks and crowding feathers
to meet my own open-and-click-closed eyes.

As the wagon pulls away,
piss pours from the back like a trail
and white feather-fluff settles on my windscreen.

A troublesome thought:

                     that my cat
has crept into the O of the washing machine
because the door is O
                    pen and it is snug in there
and O
        so
              cosy it is
to lie on clothes
              there
                    ready to wash
                    and my cat
has curled and is orange-pearled
a bit like the T-shirt
              so that
                    I don't even notice him
when I fill the dosing ball with powdered Dreft
and (of course) fling it into the very back of the O
set the machine to 40 degrees slow spin
                           slam the door
and
        off I go (perhaps) humming

and   my cat
        my cat

South Stack

For David Hart

Walking by cliff edges draws the mind to consider the various what-ifs.
We've forgotten Oscar's lead, so borrow string from Carol
for when the path dwindles and there is no wall left.
This much sea is always impressive and today, May is immaculate.
The telescope shows three thousand guillemots on rock
whitened by their being there. In a month, they'll be gone.
Amazing what detail you find when you focus.

Imagining the Full Hundred

I want to realise identity with all life,
even with such things as crawl upon earth.
GANDHI

I
Making Elderflower Cordial

Creatures can get very small –
their smallness comes as a big surprise.
These tinies are flecks of distress,
sprung pell-mell from the elder flowers
now I have squeezed the lemon juice there.

Is this earthenware bowl a scream-zone
with the creatures' pitch out of my reach?
They tumble out of petals.

As we would, too, stumble to our streets
leaving our tea tables set, our potatoes
steaming in their skins, the six o'clock news
reporting the mayhem:

> *All our skies have soured.*
> *The rain is acid enough to kill*
> *and God has been sighted*
> *wielding the sun.*

II
Armageddon

Aunty Toss shows the child
pictures of Armageddon, when God
punishes the sinners and all the saved
are saved. Craters open in the earth's crust.
Roads erupt. There is storm.

Down the cracks fall cars with faces inside.
Down the cracks fall families, this way and that.
They are paper-chain people, falling, falling
because they are sinners, and Jehovah is *cleaning up*.

The child places a smudging finger on the page,
where a brown mongrel is cartwheeling down a crack
with his family of sinners. Her own dog
peed on the carpet when he was a pup,
which probably means oh no! the Black Spot.

Will God always find you, where ever you are?
Oh yes, says the aunt. Where ever you are.

But if there's a bee in the vicinity
or a ladybird flying to her house-on-fire,
thinks the child, in not so many words.
Will they be found out for stinging,
for winging where they shouldn't?

To her aunt, she frowns. She says: I see.

III
Sprouts

When we picked our first sprouts for supper,
somebody said: *Soak them in salt water for the bugs.*
So I left them for an hour in a covered pan.

Later, when I lifted the lid, the sprouts had become
        bobbing islands in an ocean,
                on which
the dwellers had gathered, survivors of the flood.

There were slugs, worms, and baby wood lice
balanced on the backs of bigger wood lice.

        It was   a community in crisis.

        And what could I do,
gawping over the rim of that world, but become
                God?

IV
Beetle

I am sweeping the stone-slab patio, when a beetle
plummets from somewhere up and lands with a *pip*
just ahead of my broom. I home in for a look:
there are more legs than me and a shell,
but the symmetry is still recognisable.

The legs paddle the air. The beetle rocks on its back.
You can see the head working, the antennae waving.
Then, with a flip, the little someone is squat
on her feet, and ambling off towards the steps.

> *The Jains sweep at their paths*
> *and how much weeping do they do*
> *in their love for Life?*

V
Snail

Solitary snail
Skating up the window rink
One beat to the bar

Buddha-dog

your Buddha-nature shows
through your flow of expression
in daily sleep and wake

ears that listen wholly
to the minute sounds of the everyday
you do not need instruction
in watching breath
to attain focus

eyes whose language
is more eloquent than words
you are awake you are whole
hearted and realised

Buddha-dog I admit
unflinching attachment to you
and recognise the suffering
this brings
                    I do not need
meditation on death, grave yard
reminders of disintegration
                    I am well-rehearsed
in the pain that will come
at your passing
                    I accept this
                    to love you
as I accept all the sufferings
that loving brings

On such a pyre, I will be burnt to ash

I will stand any accusation
of *sentimentality*

bow-wowing low to my dog
in his lovely incarnation

Autumn is always beautiful

Without trying to solve
a thing, I sit in the afternoon
October sun and absorb
the barely stirring breeze
that rifles through the leaves
of the sweet chestnut tree.

By evening, the rains will come
and this young tree will be stripped.
A week from now, winter
will enter our lives and be long.
But now, *now*, you are alive, my friend,
and autumn is always beautiful.

Archie's moment

Archie pauses by a five bar gate to relight his pipe.
Ah Sally, he sighs, taking, for a long moment,
this dog's head in his big spadey hands.
Her eyes, old and rheumy now, like his,
never swivel away.

After rain, this is how the earth smells.
On ash leaves and alder, hedgerow and plough-land,
sunlight is falling, mottled and mutable,
and the loamy soil smells only like this.

Archie turns away from the five bar gate
the sense of nearness too much.
He whistles to dispel it
- calls his dog along -
the soft fragment of song
whose words escape him.

*From a photograph by James Ravilous
published in* Resurgence *magazine*

Ellie

For Bobby, Betty and Ruth

The yellow rose
planted in love
shimmered
on the brink
of bloom

A late frost
stole her
stopped her gold
froze her sap too soon

Now May will always
have its wound

All day

      I waited by the water
where the tree whose name I do not know
trailed branches below the river's surface

and you did not come
              though I waited

I left that place in a twilight
pinking with birdsong
and all the journey home
I thought of your
            not coming

That night, I dreamed I'd lost
my name, my face
somewhere among the detail
of the day's passing

but in the daybreak light
    I saw

    this
seemed ample seemed more
than worth the wait

Shiva's Fly

He who knows the god Shiva,
hidden in all beings, is freed from all fetters.
UPANISHADS

A fly has landed on the forehead
of the man with criss-cross socks
who cleans the face of his watch
with an off-white handkerchief.

> Wrapped in cotton, his finger
> circles the glass face, clockwise.
> He breathes – *ah* – and polishes again
> this wind-up timepiece which was his father's.

He can't get on with digital; you need
in this world hands and pointers.
Red numbers, like the ones on the wall clock,
are too self-important: executive numbers

> that rush you about. Everyone wants
> their turn to come, but he's not so bothered
> these days. His father used to say: *time's round,*
> *like your bike wheel. Ride the cycle,*

keep your balance and know when to get off.
Since his father's watch stopped, all he can feel
is *more*. This fly, for instance, on his skin,
settled now between his eyebrows.

Near-Far Shore

Must it be that I am laid so low
that I must fall in full view
in the road at the heart
of the village in full view
in the road where tarmac becomes sand
where a mirage shimmers over it like lake-water
that I upturn in I splash in I sprawl
down in the sand?
                                A deer,
shot through from some arrow,
sang from the edge of the clearing
and fell with a look of wonderment
and a gentle flow of urine
that stained the sand a small patch of yellow.

Must I too suffer this ignominy
for no reason?
                        O reason, great father of reason,
you have nothing to give but answers
that are not answers,
                                reasons
that are little more than a man
watching in his coat and hat, a spy spying
and being clever with his machinations.

The corner shop is there, the post office,
the RSPCA coin-box, the telephone kiosk
(still of the old red kind). The bank is busy,
the village is in its heyday, the bread shop,
the buttons shop and shop of ornaments
all there with their open signs and bells tinkling.

But I am lost to them.
I am from a different time,
invisible as air.
Yet the car
up by the butcher's shop,
its slow approach,
has the corporeal weight
to crush me

because I am sinking
in the sucking sand
unable to reach the far shore.

Around me, villagers are busy
buying cake and brittle toffee,
their old fashioned bicycles
propped against lamp-posts,
granary loaves in their front-baskets,
pasties, in brown paper bags,
still warm from the oven.

They don't see me
down here in the road.
They don't hear me
muffled, as I surely am, by the sand.
Only he, in the shop doorway,
in his mackintosh and dark spy's hat –
he is from my time.

So I cry out to him:
'My legs won't stand won't stand me!'
and he hears this, he hears
and while I thrash
in the sand in the road
reaching for the far shore I can't reach,
he hangs in the doorway
hands in his pockets
eyes disguised

my beholder
my witness
from my own time

and the car –
interminable, its approach.

The other side
is a place I recognise
I've been there once
there is a house with rooms
I know the feel of
there are pavements
I could stand my weight on

but my hands, their knuckles,
are white from clinging to some edge.
The fingers buckle
under the weight of holding
to the near shore,
where the villagers have gathered
to point and call
(though am I lost to them?)

and he, who waits, there
in the shop doorway
he waits

waits and waits

however long
it is a *waiting*

and in this awakening
- the relief, the release –
I raise my hands

open both palms to him
in welcome

and die like the deer
whose tears the poet sings of

and in this single act
this loosening off of grasp
faces occur in this place of sand
two four twenty more than a hundred
in this road this mid-way point of mirage
faces come, some of whom I know -
villagers, also with their bodies braced,
knuckles tight, shoulders against whatever strife
is theirs,
          and somehow I reach the far shore
as if carried
                not of my doing
and standing, I glance back towards the door-
way, knowing it, of course, now, to be empty.

On the night of the metal-work storm

On the night of the metal-work storm
with cloud-flung drama and more flooding
bound to make the news,
we sip tea and muse
about the oil running out –
is it true that it's happening,
that the earth could go west?

The lights flicker and we check for candles,
do the usual counting from the flash
to the thunder crash

nature fighting back it's what you say
across the table in a hushed voice
as the lights dip, teeter, cut

then bounce back, tenacious as life.

Red-cloud-day

In memory of Miss A

What a punch-drunk sky,
bruised like a boxer's face.
But it fits my now –
I have an ache that can't be run from.

Streaming sky, streaming time. You were visible
once you were solid I could hug you.
But you were swept
by such a current
I couldn't keep you.

I whispered all the time whispered
so you'd hear my voice it would be
the last memory, the wet words on top
of all the other times I'd said the same three things.

I notice you no longer answer my questions
preferring instead the gesture of rose
petals of perfection

which flare then fade
fall for the wind to take

After Summer

What does it mean
    to favour the poetry
of rain on sycamore?

All summer,
    I have chosen
the secret place,

where words are butterflies
    I will not net.
I can be silent for long periods –

yet I must voice myself
    at last,
natural as rain on sycamore.

Prayer Poem

In memory of Gail

Dear precious flesh, frail and needy,
this is a prayer for you.

You, the lit candle who drips your wax
and burns your length of wick, your light
both tenuous and tenacious –

You, prey to the umpteen plagues,
to draughts and gales
from the four quarters –

Know yourself, at this moment, loved –
your side
          lined with melting,
the dark
          big around you
and your little light flickering
steadfast and true.

Field

Wait in the white field
as a speck of something.
In the great white field
wait for something to start
that wasn't expected. Wait
year after year in a ritual of waiting.

*

In the great white field
a whisper
rustles through the corn like breeze –

even this maize, rooted in chemical soil,
this utilitarian cash-crop
destined for the intensive feed trough

yes

it too has the song hushing through its stalks
its sunny kernels can't help but be
gold in certain uncertain light

*

The names of the green world –
an inheritance I did not inherit.
Each generation grows further from the land.
I must teach myself the poetry of names
- campion, cowslip, white sticky catchfly –
colours of the many in the great white field.

*

When coming to sing
first
you must listen.

In all the din
of the machine world,
listen for the deep sound.

*

In this field, weeds are an affliction.
They steal nourishment light water
they steal space money time (is money)
mess up the steady lines

We say weeds
to avoid the detail
of naming
which takes us too close

*

The names of the green world -
an inheritance I did not inherit.
I must teach myself the poetry of weeds:
- melancholy thistle, celandine -
colours of the many in the great white field.

*

Music is in the listening -
how much can you take?
I'm sorry I forgot you for that moment
when the wind
sounded the sycamores.

*

Green is not a single colour.
We say grass thinking
we explain ourselves.
Nouns are a configuration
on the white page
we fix meaning to.

*

Weed = pest
for which
there is always
a solution
ending in *-cide*

*

Change weed to herb
in four moves -

weed: heed: herd: herb.

Creative solutions
can be possible
at every instance.

*

The names of the green world –
an inheritance I did not inherit.
I must teach myself the poetry of herbs
– calendula, selfheal, St John's Wort –
colours of the many in the great white field.

*

When rain comes at last
after the long drought -

when the rain comes,
it comes not as expected,
not as a tempest
with timpani rolls
and histrionic arrows of electric charge

when it comes
when it comes
it just
comes

*

All forms are possible
at every instance.
No shape is an outcast.
The mind need only accept

banking cloud to the west bringing rain,
after-shine of leaves, light on slate roofs
and, at the end of the same day,
rose-fire in the windows of Ty Mawr.

Green Fragment

And they found themselves at last
in the garden of the long afternoon
two acorns dropped from the Great Oak
becoming rooted, roots reaching
down into the earth, sapling branches
growing through each other
up towards the light

Acknowledgements

John Howard Moore, *The Universal Kinship*, 1906.

'Picnic on Ajman Beach' published in *New Welsh Review and Teaching a Chicken to Swim*, ed. Rob Middlehurst (Seren, 2000).

'Mother (who can't swim)' published in *Iron* and *Teaching a Chicken to Swim*, ed. Rob Middlehurst (Seren, 2000).

'The Dog Shoot' published in *Stand*.

'Stonefish' published in *Teaching a Chicken to Swim*, ed. Rob Middlehurst (Seren, 2000).

'When you lived in Jamaica, Mum' published in *Poetry Wales*.

'Cousin in a Strange Land' published in *Staple*.

'Rock Fancies Movement' published in *New Welsh Review and Teaching a Chicken to Swim*, ed. Rob Middlehurst (Seren, 2000).

'Sonnet for Gorwel' published in *New Welsh Review* and *Anglesey Anthology* ed. Dewi Roberts (Gwasg Carreg Gwalch, 1999).

'Boxing with Shadows' published in *Obsessed with Pipework*.

'Another Annunciation' published in *Staple*.

'That Last Week' published in *Scintilla*.

'Making Tea, November 4th' published in *Poetry Wales*.

'Bonfire Night' published in *Poetry Wales and Anglesey Anthology*, ed. Dewi Roberts (Gwasg Carreg Gwalch, 1999).

'Hay-making in Capel Gwyn' published in *Anglesey Anthology*, ed. Dewi Roberts (Gwasg Carreg Gwalch, 1999).

'Oscar' published in *Skald*.

'A Heavily Accented Pause' published in *Skald* and *New Welsh Review*.

'South Stack' published in *Obsessed with Pipework*.

'Aunt' published in *Planet*.

'Field' published in *Planet*.

'Red-cloud-day' published in O*bsessed with Pipework*.

'Ellie' published in *Obsessed with Pipework*.

'A Troublesome Thought' published in *Obsessed with Pipework*.

'Brother Francis' published in *Obsessed with Pipework*.

'Near-Far Shore' published in *Fire*.

'Imagining the Full Hundred':
(i) This sequence is published in the anthology *Needs Be*, ed. David Hart (Flarestack,1998) under the title 'Obsessing over Small Things'.
(ii) 'Imagining the full hundred' is a line from a poem by David Hart entitled 'The snail sets out up the steps' in *Setting the Poem to Words* (Five Seasons Press, 1998).

'Shiva's Fly' was a commissioned poem for 'Waiting Rooms', a national project supported by the Poetry Society and sponsored by the Arts Council of England and the King's Fund. The editing poets were Rogan Wolf and David Hart.

With thanks to all the above editors for their support.